PATIENT ZERO

Tomás Q. Morín

Patient Zero

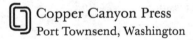

Copper Canyon Press
Port Townsend, Washington

Copper Canyon Press is in residence at Fort Worden State Park in Port Townsend, Washington, under the auspices of Centrum. Centrum is a gathering place for artists and creative thinkers from around the world, students of all ages and backgrounds, and audiences seeking extraordinary cultural enrichment.

LIBRARY OF CONGRESS CATALOGING-IN-PUBLICATION DATA
Names: Morín, Tomás Q., author.
Title: Patient zero / Tomás Q. Morín.
Description: Port Townsend, WA : Copper Canyon Press, [2017]
Identifiers: LCCN 2016050457 | ISBN 9781556594939 (paperback)
Subjects: | BISAC: POETRY / American / Hispanic American.
Classification: LCC PS3613.O7542 A6 2017 | DDC 811/.6—dc23
LC record available at https://lccn.loc.gov/2016050457

Copper Canyon Press
Post Office Box 271
Port Townsend, Washington 98368
www.coppercanyonpress.org

For Philip Levine

CONTENTS

PATIENT ZERO

NATURE BOY

If I had enough cages to keep all the birds
I've collected over the years then I would have
to open a shop because there's only so much room
in a two-bedroom walk-up for 48 birds,
not to mention the dancing bears and the frogs,
or the different varieties of fish, the one
species of flea, and I almost forgot the proud
dogs and the lone mule, the profane one
who entered my life to curse at scribes and pharisees;
and maybe he'd let the mouse I found
forever dying at the end of a poem
ride on his back like a whiskered Christ
and if not, maybe my yeti could do it
when he's not downtown working
security at the store or teaching the parrots
how to say *brotherhood* in grunt
and how to comb out the tangles and mud
from his hair, whose sweat reminds me
of that bearded collector of beasts
with the ark who would have no doubt
understood how I feel, that prophet
of change under whose spell I want to confess
that I'm a Christian of the Old Testament,
that my grandfather hung all his goats
upside down, their throats over a bucket,
and slapped their chests like that other Nature Boy
who strutted around the ring
like a peacock with his feathered hair
that stayed immaculate

even on the nights he lost to our hero
Wahoo McDaniel who never played the heel,
he who hailed from the lost tribes
of Oklahoma, who made us want to be chiefs
so much we wore pigeon feathers
and circled each other inside a green square
of water hose until someone finally rang the bell
that was never there and we sprang
toward each other like animals in love or at war.

SAUDADES

When that word, one part swine,
one part evasion, first wobbled into my life
I was eating pastrami and hiding in my office
from students and I know Andrade was in the air,
as was the samba, and how it's almost impossible
to translate either one, nor should you
unless you've been a disciple of the rough grief
that lovingly wraps you in its wings, which is warmer
than one would expect, so much so that it's easy
to forget for a moment something trivial like pigs
aren't supposed to fly or that if you say *saudades*
with enough pain and heart the pigs of your past will come
trotting out of the dark, doing their little sideways dance
around you, shaking their hips to the drum
in your chest until you forget what a frown is
or why we need them and oh they will remind you
how delicious Carnival is, and how glorious
it is to make the past present, and how
easily one can sleep dressed in feathers.

NUDIST COLONY

Wind-whipped, ear-clapped
by the rocky thunder of the coast,
they cross the wet grass
in burnished loafers, sandals

twined on the grounds
to drink and merrymaking.
Inland, they face the empty
hour between lunch

and dinner in a frail
building with a barking
door and incandescent
lighting that wraps the matte

surface of their trunks
in an amber glow. Sheets
of paper shuffle, chalk
boxes are laid out,

oils are stirred, sharpened
pencils line up in formation,
hips swivel and settle
on wooden stools

legged in metal. She
enters and her shoes click
across the white tile
as she assumes the center

of the room in a pencil skirt
and matching jacket, taupe
blouse and run stocking.
Her husband sets a flock

of gooseflesh up his neck
and starts to chalk her legs
from memory: his first
black dash and swipe

might be an eel
beached on blanched rock
but for the second
slash against the page

that frames the long thigh
and the knot of the knee.
She shifts her weight
from one foot to the next,

scarlet-heeled, toe tips
white with pressure.
Soft rock in hand,
he drags it slow

on a fresh wall of white
and applies the pressure
necessary to make her
more than a pool

of smudges and parts.
Wet clay in the corner

begins to harden
and blended watercolors

matte the predrawn
run of the ribs,
the swaddled shoulders
grained in autumn

tones like the disrobed
grasses in drains
that suffer cold-scald
and wind-jag.

The wrists busy now
lashing and hooking
hair to the scalp,
skin-cap to the face,

drifting shallow wrinkles
at the eye-pinch,
southerly to the ear,
leveled around the neck

like the soft-piled lines,
ruddy-pale-white,
on the brassy cheek
of the dusk-christened cliffs.

WEEKEND HOME

Not like any of the solemn ones on the cape
sitting empty week after week on those
ice-bitten January streets one can never find

in summer magazines and I am tempted, as with
so many things, to say a house can grow
a conscience when no one is around to slam its

wooden tongues and I wonder if it'll miss
the romantic declarations of our long nights
spent sobbing and roaring, promising the end

of the end of love, and how I so wanted to see
the face it made when we slowly pulled out
of the driveway for the last time I never

shared out of meekness until now; was it a Garbo
pleading for adoration or a wrinkled Rimbaud
for melancholy, because with much effort

we had done what we do best and put away
another season of anger in the books, made healthy
our tab with another debt we could never repay.

THE SHORE PARTY

The grill sits with its mouth open
like a child begging for more.
I've lost count of the franks we've eaten

and the beer we've downed. My wife floats
in the water with her friends, their white skin
striped red. When a boat speeds by,

a false tide bobs them like buoys,
and for a while the old conversations
about love lost/found, the fickle

needs of lovers, are replaced with laughter.
Listening to them I'm given a second life
in which I forget the friends I no longer have,

those lost to time, the ones given up to distance.
Not wanting to lose what I now have,
I plot a wooden frame

around our square of lake,
its legs sunk deep in the sandy bottom,
the far end open to the water,

east and west a window
(maybe curtains, too); a dock
stretches from the lip of the bank

into the boathouse where hunger will knock,
where winter will sleep.
When I come to my senses, the sad

box where I would have kept them
like singing mermaids gives way
to the aimless mind of the wind

teasing the junipers, skimming
the brown surface of the green water,
nudging the black tubes of the tight circle

of sisters who are not sisters
whose hearts I cannot save. I slip out
of my shirt and shoes. As I wade in

I raise my hand in a sort of wave
as the cold water teaches me humility,
as I deepen the melody of their laughter.

CIRCUS PONY

What joy to say our short winter days
are behind us now. Gone the old life we filled
with empty laughter, the times we'd pack
the backseat with every hitchhiking clown
we happened upon — our record was eight
— until the year our fathers died. Gone
the red-nosed hours, our grotesque smiles
drawn large and wide, when we rehearsed
our cold routines of "Hey, are you okay?" and "Fine.
I'll be fine." Remember the long seconds — three
slow ones in all — before your face
that took an hour to apply turned grave
or the look you wore, sadder than any clown's
in the rain, that was my cue to knit my brow
and continue fumbling with the three-sizes-too-small
hammer you handed me so I could once more fix
the swaybacked rocking horse we purchased
to ward off an unspoken future in which we
are continents apart, surrounded by our hungry
new families as we slice and dismantle
the same braised roast and lament how
we could have let hope stray, how the story
of our lives might have been different
if it had contained, however lame, something
we could have ridden into the sunset on.

PATIENT ZERO

Love is a worried, old heart
disease, as Son House once put it, the very stuff
blues are made of, real blues
that consist of a male and female, not monkey junk
like the "Okra Blues" or "Payday Blues,"
though I think House would agree
two hearts of any persuasion are enough for a real blues,
if one of them is sick, that sickly green of a frog
bitten in two by the neighbor's dog, all of which
makes me wonder about the source of our disease
and whose teeth first tore the heart after Adam
and Eve left the garden. Some have argued
that the first case of infection
could be traced to a carp or a stork, or maybe
even the hare, because God made them first, after all,
but the love lives of birds and fish,
even rough rabbit love, are more perfect
in their simplicity than we can ever hope to know
such do they dispense with the rituals
of courtship in short order
so much so we don't really want to admit
the beasts and fowl and all manner of slithery thing
can truly love like us
so we label the heat of their hearts
and loins "affection" or "instinct"
or some trick of the lower brain and I think
if we are to be good scientists we must investigate
the moment when the sons of God made themselves
known to the daughters of men

before we turn up a singer strumming
a lute shaped like the goose egg
the singer's mouth makes
every time she bends the long, mournful note
about how her angel traded his feathers
so he could walk in the skin of God's prize creation
and in so doing became the first man she ever knew
who wasn't full of shit
and yet was, because even though angels never eat,
her holy birdman always hemmed and hawed
when she asked point-blank
why it always took him so long to fetch a gallon
of moonlight or why he kept his wings
folded and why is it he wouldn't crow
her name to the dawn unless the night
before she had said, *Enough is enough, we're done,*
and her face had flooded and his
chest had burned cold
until the dark cracked and let a light creep through
to which he opened up and sang
in a tongue she didn't understand but did
just enough to know their sickness
was something, and divine, and endless.

LOVE TRAIN

for D'Andra

My bowl brimming with pretzels,
the snack you wanted least,
I slid open the door of our sleeping car
where we had been enjoying the country rushing by,
as if we were the first two people
to look down into the valleys and see
bright necks of pines stretch across farms
and streams to the groves they once cradled.
You had asked for Earl Grey cookies
sandwiched around buttercream or marshmallows
made of chocolate, but all the tea bags had been dunked
and the chocolate melted over biscotti.
When I came bearing the salted and twisted news,
the room was empty but for a heel. It was black
as a bunting, and wound with zippers,
and every time the car rocked
it looked ready to fly and escape
into the cold, tangled air
of travel that always feels heavy
with joy and desire, and a little sadness,
always a little sadness,
because of the leaving, which is what I do
when I realize I'm in the wrong room
and that numbers have betrayed me again
while I was hunting and gathering,

foraging like *Homo habilis*
who probably never lost his cave.

Out of patience, I opened every door
marked with threes and eights, those conjoined twins
disastrously separated at birth,
and roused the scabbed eyes of sleepers
like a beggar, no, an angel,
a begging angel who has written on his heart
WILL WORK FOR LOVE.
Having not found our room, not heard
the sharp swing of your voice,
I descended upon the passenger cars
and row upon row of couples asleep
or staring out the windows like zombies
trying to remember what happens next
once the newspaper is well thumbed,
the tea has gone cold, and the conversation is dead.

I called for you, in vain, even using your secret names,
the ones only the night knows:
wind-kiss, brilliant-fruit, dervish-moon...
Over and over, I said your names,
over and over until they filled
the wounded air of the car
and when there was no more room
for another sound, they caught and hooked
the ring of the brakes hugging the rails.

Just when I thought I wouldn't find you,
you were there, the train was pulling away,
and I was watching you slowly eat

a dish of whipped cream and bananas
—the house special—in a café
in a city we didn't know.

When you finished, we started walking
down a road that bent like a smile,
a shy smile, like the one the Japanese cat wore
on your purse. The road, we were told,
would take us to the end of the line
where all lovers in search of joy
packed on bullet trains—they're the fastest
on two continents—arrive every hour.

CALLE A CALLE

So I am tired of being a man.
So I go to the tailor shops and the movies
worn out, impervious, like a felt swan
navigating a sea of creation and ash.

The smell of the barbershops makes me bawl.
All I want is the peace of stones or wool,
all I want is to see no more stores or gardens,
no more merchandise, or glasses, or elevators.

So I am tired of my feet and my nails
and my hair and my shadow.
So I am tired of being a man.

All the same it would be delightful
to scare an accountant with a cut lily
or kill a nun with a blow to the ear.
It would be beautiful
to go through the streets with a green knife
and shout until I froze to death.

I don't want to continue as a root in the dark,
hesitant, stretched out, shivering from night sweats,
down below, in the wet bowels of the earth,
soaking it up and thinking, eating each day.

I don't want all this misery.
I don't want to continue as a root and a tomb,

always underground, as a cellar of freezing
corpses, dying of my own self-pity.

That is why Monday burns like oil
when it sees me arrive with my cage of a face,
and why it howls like a wounded wheel as it passes,
and why it makes tracks of hot blood toward night.

And it shoves me into certain corners, certain damp houses,
hospitals where bones spill out of the windows,
certain shoe stores that smell like vinegar,
onto streets as frightening as chasms.

There are birds the color of sulfur and horrible intestines
hanging from the doors of the houses I hate,
there are dentures forgotten in a coffeepot,
there are mirrors
that should have wept from shame and fear,
there are umbrellas everywhere, and poison, and navels.

I walk around calmly, with eyes, with shoes,
with anger, forgetful,
I pass, I cross offices and orthopedic stores,
and courtyards where laundry hangs from a wire:
underwear, towels, and shirts that weep
long dirty tears.

translated from the Spanish of Pablo Neruda

AT THE SUPERMARKET

What have I forgotten? Milk for bones —
Salt for blood — A fresh loaf
for sleep. Outside, Sunday morning
has expired. The line is long
for this hour. When the doors open
the squawks of gulls blown too far inland
announce nothing is impossible. The cashier
vanishes again for the cigarette key
and the moment slows the way moments do
when the eye is fixed for too long —:
the man in front of me smells tart,
like solder; a woman's clutch
blurs into the business end of a rabbit,
while her blond son negotiates
a landslide of candy. Before my eyes
water and wash away the fog, a hand,
mottled indigo like a map of archipelagoes,
brushes my lettuce as the man behind me
leans forward to say, "Would you look at that?"
On the cover of a magazine, a man is bound;
above him, a white metal bowl
trimmed in navy, big enough to wash an infant in;
from within, a sheer, crystalline arm
reaches down the page to the pit of his mouth;
in the foreground, his stomach swells
pale over the words, manifest in a slanted,
judicial font: *What Can Water Cure?*
"Look, like a froggie," the boy giggles,
pleased to have discovered something familiar.

His mother, shocked, covers his mouth
and whispers about their box of ice cream,
praline I think, that is already sweating.

If we were trapped in a Rockwell,
the boy would be on his knees
with a ladder truck, imagining all the fire ants
he would douse and save from themselves.
And his hero's face would be grim and grave
like the gorilla slung from a pole
on the *National Geographic*.
And because love is better shared,
there would be a sister for the boy,
clutching her wooden doll, whose arms
join deep within her maple body
to a single peg so that she can only cheer
and mime *rah rah rah* with the thick red *O*
drawn where her nose should be.
An exotic cigar juts from a jeweler's mouth
—is this me? Or am I the carpentered parrot
clutching a ring, drawn toward the door
and the dull horizon that is always itself,
no matter how jungled his dreams?

"What?" I say, then, "Oh, yes, horrible..."
in that blunt, exasperated voice we perfect
during times like this. The conveyor resumes
with a jolt and my cherry tomatoes,
the last of the heirloom season, roll
from their bag toward the awful laser eye
we are taught to avoid lest one go blind.
(This must be what it's like to be seen

by God: a lidless light sunk in the dark
scanning the soul.) Now beer, now crackers — ;
the girl totals and totals what we owe,
as we inch and inch toward the infinite.

On dirt-packed roads that thinned and fell apart
like breath in winter, we sputtered along
in our car, a yellow coupe with a memory
for recording groves of myrtle and secular pine
in kilometers. For six days we milled around forts,
bays, and bare, gold dunes stormed and conquered
too often to accurately count
on the island shaped like a foot, no, the print
of a foot — God's, in fact.
Or so the locals say.
At the rough southern tip
where the limestone runner's heel
would have first struck, we break bread
at the wobbly table we've claimed as our own
for the last time and take in every detail:
the sleepy violets on the table,
the handmade menus that smell like fish,
which is to say fresh
off the boat, and the waiter,
the lanky one missing teeth
whose mouth sounds like a piano
tuned for serenades,
who is flirting with you
while I sit and grin
as I imagine Odysseus must have grinned
at his wife's bold suitors
because we are in the birthplace
of the dropwort, after all, that sweet
ditch-daisy Carthaginians brewed

for criminals and the elderly,
who, knowing no better, drank it
and danced as their faces twisted
into a smile Socrates would have known,
that tender old clown
who saw the humor in death,
who would have seen the wisdom
of spending the last of our jigsawed days
feasting and raising our glasses
to the most merciful god of glee
until laughter did us part.

CARITÀ AMERICANA

I found regret in a deli case;
it was white and shaped like a brick.
On the label a cow from Vermont
grazed on forget-me-nots or drank
from a pond. I can't remember which,
since it was the black splatters
— or was it white splotches —
I was taken with, and the thin legs,
and the elegant body shaped like a tank.
Although, what I remember most
is the missing udder, that pink fist
of gravity every Holstein swings,
whose absence could have been intended
because the artist hoped liberating his cows
from the bondage of breasts
(an act of charity, no doubt,
though not Roman; Hindu, maybe)
would impress the feminist he was dating
who was head over heels
for vegan babka.

The meatcutter offered me a taste,
because he saw how I kept staring
longingly in his case (as if I were starving)
at that blessèd cow without nipples
drawn by a lovesick artist in Jersey
who wanted me to believe it gave the milk
that made the immaculate cheese
now sitting in my hand,

whose taste I already knew well,
even though I played the naïf, even though
I knew better, that after I had chewed the last bite
of that sacred square, in two minutes' time,
maybe less, I would begin expanding,
but not with the Holy Ghost,
with lactose, in the small intestine,
so that by the time I reached my car
I'd be ready for the fiddle
because I would look like one of the demented
Roman emperors, the ones that were all paunch
and wild eyes and who had a taste for fire.

To the young meatcutter waiting
for my answer, for 5 o'clock, for an escape
from the madness of fluorescent lighting,
I wanted to say *Thou,* wanted to be formal,
not because it rhymed with *cow,*
it was that magical beast after all that joined us,
but because we were beyond the quotidian now,
and biblical time is archaic
and thus it would only be proper to say, "Thou
slicer, Thou priest of the cold cut
who set me on the path
of suffering with an act of charity,
do you know your Vermeer, your Caravaggio
and Rubens, and thus the story
of Pero and Cimon, and how the one,
the grown child, fed the other,
her jailed father, in secret, with the milk
of her body, so that he wouldn't die
as had been decreed, from want, from lack

of food and drink,
and how when all was discovered
the father was released and the daughter's gift
was named *Carità Romana*?"

I mumble, "Thou, Thou," and then,
"No, thanks," because I'm already late
to visit my father in the hospital,
in his cold room that, in another country,
one thick with forests and secrets,
with caves to hide in from the authorities,
would be for enemies of the state.
He's a prisoner of his body
— his hunger is vulgar, beastly even,
but unlike Pero, there is no milk in my chest,
which I would let him cleave and suckle anyway
but for the bitterness swimming there.
He looks almost Roman now
with his buzzed head and marching veins.
For all his brio, he'll never teach another son
how to steal corn by moonlight,
just enough to eat and sell,
or how to build a house, or how to read
the soot marks on any brick
from the great Chicago fire of 1871.

When he wakes and adds his lowing
baritone to the shrieks and trills
of his neighbors down the hall,
I clear my throat and do my best cowbird
and watch his face cloud
with yearning, a naked shyness,

like the kind a calf wears
when it's startled by your voice
and it drops its mother's nipple to stare at you,
milk still hot on its tongue.
His sweet cow face is almost enough
for me to forget the old injuries,
how he laughed every time I retched
in the bathroom because of the butter
he hid in my food. No, I can't lie
and tell him what he wants to hear,
will not say that I love him, will not
admit to that. Instead, I'll wash his hair
and clip his nails, shave his face,
and when my traitorous lip trembles
with pity, I'll whistle
louder, longer, and teach him about regret,
feed it to him one note at a time,
and though he knows he shouldn't,
he'll devour it with the knowledge
that my song will swell and split his heart.

SALAD DAYS

for Micah Ruelle

We were not green in judgment or cold
in blood like Cleopatra in her youth
who still was ordering chopped radish
in her bowls back then,
the hearts all gone to pieces
next to the winter greens
that in our days we never had use for
so smitten were we with fire
and ovens that I was gravy in judgment,
which might not mean much
unless you've taken a spoon
of it and poured it back over a dumpling
shaped like your heart
so that it became even softer,
something you could not have thought possible.
It's all happening now,
you liked to say, and I agreed,
though it was not the news
from the outside I relished,
but the daily *Extra! Extra!* the light
of the morning brought to my attention
every time we woke in your house
or my house and my heart
— salty, risen — was warm
again in a way it hadn't been for years.
Organ of reason, organ of righteousness
that has never had a single flavor cross its lips,
how could you know

how much I would miss the honey of those days,
her drizzle of it on the turkey bacon,
my cracking pepper up and down the pan,
the sweet meat of happiness
I would no longer let pass between our teeth.

THE FOOD CRITIC

My beat is the restaurant,
the diner, the chophouse. On any day,
without calling ahead,
I'm whisked into a plush booth
lit by fresh, white bulbs
gauzed in yellow. My picture,
an old photo probably cut
from a book, hangs
in every kitchen in town
next to the garlic and knives.
Two, maybe three, fit waiters
will taxi plates and flood
the crumbling chains of ice in my glass.

Food is truly the best subject
for a poet. At least we were told that
when books went away.
Few of us could believe it
when we were given a paycheck
and an audience. Now, no more rhymes
or pretty books with pretty names.
But, it's not as bad as it sounds.
There are worse things
than being one of the acknowledged
legislators of taste.
Just think of the poor novelist

who must write movies or obituaries;
there's little difference, I'm told.

For the masses, I dine
on both the good and the bad. In Reno
I ate a street bird—pigeon,
I think it was—that tasted like tobacco,
with dry brown rice
and just-picked beans fresh
enough to pop between your teeth.
Once, I sliced a rib eye
in Omaha, bone-out, so tender
it blinked like a cat.

This is the kingdom
we have inherited. Happiness
is a solemn slice of black-tie cake
waiting in every hotel room,
while grief is missing the pyramids
of donut burgers and Twinkies
after your funeral. And love,
well, love is still the first law
of the land
because what else is a double scoop
of bacon ice cream
if not a monument to self-love?
Now, every poet is a love poet,
which should be cause for celebration
because every editorial, column, and review
is now a love letter, a valentine

like this one
I've just typed for you,
>Hungry Reader:

Where the unswept walkways of
the streets convene and jut into a
soiled T tattooed on the face of
the horn-brown waters a boat with
the bones of a house rocks. Where
a dozen odd rows of riveted steel
benches once held whale watch-
ers like penitents, where a gener-
ation earlier deckhands briskly
scrubbed the sop of viscera, forty
may comfortably dine. Two hun-
dred and fifty-five green-black
bottles of globe-trotting grapes
stacked like the dead lie in repose
off the kitchen. Corralled by win-
dows, from any table the city rises
coal-grey and rotten in the west
like broken fingers on an untended
hand. Eastward, the pitiless ocean
laps the cold hull out of which a
dumbwaiter ascends with disks
of fried crab in horseradish pud-
dles. Glazed Berlin venison is the
special, roasted with authentic
wall-climbing wild carrots. Double-
barreled cherry blintzes mark the
end of the meal and the violet
bruise of a late sky.

<table>
<tr><td>53</td></tr>
<tr><td><h1>Ai</h1>愛 小川
191</td></tr>
</table>

NAME

Love. Ai Ogawa. 愛 小川. Small River of Love.
1(A) + 9(i) = 10 = Spirit Force. Florence Anthony.

ATOMIC NUMBER

53[1]

ATOMIC WEIGHT

191[2]

MELTING POINT

Unknown. Clear and cool, just as in the dark deep of the cavernous dirt from where it springs. In tests has withstood the heat of fame, ridicule, an Oklahoma sun, not to mention the fire of shame and poverty, as well as the flames of men.

BOILING POINT

Repeated classification as Irish, Black, Choctaw-Chickasaw, Japanese, Comanche, Southern Cheyenne, ½ this, ⅛ that, or any combination one can rename and claim as their own.

---

1. number of years lived
   minus the number of books published.
2. total number of poems
   collected in all books less
   repeats in volumes selected and collected.

Sin Eater. Baptism. Oracle. First discovered in 1973. People wade into a small river of love and it is like entering a killing floor. The water, while cool, burns until hate peels off your body and floats away in strips. Once your skin is gone and your marbled rage exposed, re-submerge and let all that swims pick you clean. After the river has fed on you, float and let the sun smile on your slaughter. This is the rest of your reward. The first of it was given under the surface when your screams meant you at last had come to know love by its other names.

DANCE COUPLE

"As the explosive spins away from his chest
it's out with the tired step-ball-change…"

In my dumb youth
I would have made the plastique male,
and French, a devotee of fashion,
would have recklessly decked it in a bubble dress
because bombs are round in cartoons. Later,
after making love, I would have returned
and unrolled fishnets — white, always white
— up its murderous thighs to simulate the crisp twine
the violence depends upon. Baghdad
would've become a chic disco grinding
the night into submission for the sublime
parade of Halstons and Qianas.

Beauty is for suckers,
I overheard a man mumble in the park,
his handsome bow tie crooked, while the pug
tethered to his hand lifted one noble leg
in salute to the awful carnation.
I am done with beauty, I thought,
with perfuming the wounds of the world
and so I retreat to the ugly heart,
that unpopulated, suspended
acre of island, where, at the right time of year,
one can walk unmolested the miles
and miles of beach and hear nothing.
Once in a great while, the foul tide

will drag a frond, brown and tattered,
into the current. From far below
its saw-shaped outline will appear like a feather
from some giant bird to the sea spiders,
translucent, faithfully
following their own cancerous rhythm
into the bloody dark of the heart
where they will spin and spin
the death of our couple, given time.

SING SING

She had lived within
    the white stone walls

so long she couldn't
    remember any longer

the face of the man
    who ferried her across

the river. When she tried
    to see him she saw

nothing. What struck her
    always about that night

was how from the boat
    the black crest of beech

and maples joined the
    dark flat of the river

to make a green yawn
    each second made

yawn even wider.
    She never could forget

this coupling of solid
    and liquid darks so

unbroken and total except
        where the buildings sat

locked arm in arm
        along the shore.

The ferryman had said
        on a night like this,

when stars were dim, one
        could look at the savage

light of those buildings and
        swear it was the harvest moon

dipping for a drink.
        For years her pride

had kept her from begging
        a parole board of strangers

for mercy and a little
        tenderness. But now

she was finally tired
        of walls and it was time

to acknowledge her crimes
        and apologize so she took

the sheet of grey
        paper she had folded

to look like the gull
      wheeling overhead,

and flattened it. Her hair
      firmly tucked behind her ear,

she sighed and wrote:

    Esteemed
parole board, I've
spent every hour
wondering what I could
have done differently,
how things might've
turned out if I hadn't
broken the rules and
followed my poet out
of the house and away
from the page. I was sure
he was going to abandon
his words for what would've
been the 10th time
since he believed he had
no talent to speak of,
that the future readers
of America, dull and
overfed on vampire
poetry, would shred his
"stupid poems" and sell
them by the bag
as packing material. He
couldn't write about

the dead South anymore
or the war between the races.
I was sure not a soul
would know I was watching
him as he slid a sack
over his leg and the
leg of a woman he didn't
know loved him yet.
How could I know
when I tripped them so
he could fall on her
and they could roll and laugh
that she would die? I was
supposed to make him a poet
of joy, not grief.

          She
stopped writing
      and stared away

at the bleached stones
      of the wall stacked

like loaves of bread.
      Walls this high, she'd

learned, had a way
      of making the mind

forget what was real
      so that before you knew it,

you were staring hard
        enough to misremember

your own father
        shuffling in the kitchen —

a tune playing on his lips —
        from mixing bowl to oven

and back again until all
        the sills and countertops

and tables were heavy
        with golden bread he braided.

Those warm slices she
        never tasted bubbled up

in the soup of her
        mind when the steam

from the laundry room
        slipped down the corridors

or when sweat clinging
        to hair met the hot pillow

on the bed below her. A wall
        built high and plain enough

could easily bend
        a memory, is meant to,

which is why so few
        ever remember the past

true enough to know what
        they're apologizing for.

Because she knew the land
        the prison was built on once

belonged to the Sint Sinck
        tribe who fished and camped

the shores, the white
        stones of the wall

were only ever stones
        and nothing more.

But her apology couldn't be
        about forgetting. She knew this,

knew she must tell the past
        true if she were ever to grow

a seed of sympathy
        in anyone's heart

and so she started again
        and wrote:

                Ladies
and gentlemen, I present

the facts of my life: before
I was a Muse, milk
and cheese were my trade
by day, a warped
fiddle by night. I sawed
the most bent notes
a Kansas City sky
ever did hear. Five
years later I was kissing
strangers at the carnival
for a nickel a piece.
I was inspiring them
to kiss their wives
harder. Yes, I'll admit,
long in the tooth couples
necking in a Buick
isn't art, but wouldn't
you rather see that
than the high drama
divorce on the lawn
of a courthouse? How
I came to inspire a poet
from the South hell
bent on writing love
poems about Roman
gods and goddesses
I can't recall. Four more
weeks and I would've cured
him of the silly idea
of gods. Love, now
there's godliness
in that idea. For the record,

I never was a god. I am
spirit same as you,
moving body to body
through the years, always
sneaking into the background
of people's lives when
they need focus the most,
which is all inspiration
really is. Drown out
the noise of your life
miraculously one day
and rest assured I'll be
mowing grass or snoring
on the couch in a key
so pure the busy world
slows down clear
enough for you to finally
see and hear what was
always there.

                   She looked
         at what she had written

and knew it was wrong.
        She'd said too much

about the nature of things.
        People of most stripes

prefer their beauty simple,
        she thought. Most want to see

a crest of beech and maple
    as perfectly clearly in the dark

as in the day, not the shifting
    black crouching like a dog

about to leap across
    the water. A hill is a hill

is true enough, but how
    many prisoners had forgotten

over the years this simple
    truth on their ferry ride

and been smothered almost
    to death by the warm dog breath

of the shore and emptied
    their dinner into the Hudson?

She had to omit the past
    if she were to have a chance,

leave out all her years
    of hard work. She couldn't

mention all the singers
    and politicians, doctors

and artists, who built
    with her help great pain

into art. No one had cared
        about any of this at sentencing

and no one at her parole
        hearing would care either.

The future was where
        she needed to focus

so she crossed out
        everything she had written

and wrote:

                Dear officers
of the court, if you see
fit to release me, I
pledge to inspire
responsibly or not at all.
If it's my luck to draw
another southerner
obsessed with pie
and ribs and sun-soaked
tea, I'll nurture her
natural inclinations
toward food until feasts
complete with appetizers
and desserts spring
from her pages. And
if it's sports she loves
more than anything, she'll
have the great lacrosse

players of the Hudson
valleys crisscrossing
her canvases. I won't
repeat my mistakes
from the past. I'll give
in to every whim
and indulge the people
who need me. If another
poet selling jewelry
to snobs from the suburbs
to make a living goes
out on a limb and asks
a bookbinder from
Tennessee who is
also a closet poet
if he wants to partner
with her for the sack races
celebrating Washington
Irving Day, I'll stand
to the side and let nature
follow whatever crooked
course it cares to go.
If you see me fit
to walk free I'll find
her parents and nudge them
to take up singing
lessons. Nudge them
to wail, to howl to the stars
with perfect pitch about
their great misfortune.
And him, him I'll...

The shadow

of the lost gull sounding
        overhead kept crossing her lap

as it shrank against the empty
        blue that on a clear day like today

was like a second river
        that didn't suffer the traffic

of ferries and whose
        shores waited for nothing.

When sleep would not come
        she lay in bed thinking

about the gulls that would get lost
        in the valley. Even though

she knew it would not help,
        she closed her eyes

and flew up the warm
        face of the Palisades

before rising still higher
        and then flying downriver,

her wings still as she
        let the current of wind catch

and carry her past Nyack
      and Dobbs Ferry, Yonkers

and Manhattan, Hoboken
      and Red Hook, down to

where the river empties,
      where the breakers

crash and toss and their
      old groan is washed and

drowned in the dusky song
      of a thousand happy gulls

hissing and squalling. As the
      light grew weaker the shadow

of the gull cutting across
      the yard stretched into

the shape a child's kite
      would make. She had a son,

the woman who died.
      He would be older now,

maybe even a father.
      Promising to be responsible

would not be enough.
      She'd have to say

what they wanted, what
        her lawyer had begged

her to say all along
        to prove she wasn't crazy.

For her own protection
        she scratched through

all her words until they
        were unreadable, balled up

the paper and tossed it
        on the ground and began

a fresh page with what
        she knew they wanted

to hear:

        Fellow citizens,
I'm the same as you
in that I was reared
right by decent parents.
They mourned me
good and proper
the summer I lit out
of Iowa with a carnival.
Ten years it took
to work up to an act
in the big tent. My talent
was confidence, pure

and simple, though
I wrote FORTUNE
on my banner. The old
timers called it a knack
for knowing the heart
of people. All I had
to do was decide what
they wanted and give them
a little push in the direction
they were already headed.
I got so used to calling
myself special I forgot
to stop after the carnival
and I split. Confused
is what I was. I see
clearly now. I'm a woman
who broke the law,
plain and simple. The only
thing special about me
today is I have a debt
that needs paying. If
you see your way to grace
me with a chance to enter
the world again, I pledge
to be like a struck
match in the dark
and light the way for those
who are lost from the path
of good citizenry.
You have my word
and faith.

Her tucked hair

slipped loose from her ear.
　　　She left it to sickle

under her jaw, smiled
　　　at what she had written

and then rose and left
　　　the almost empty yard

to keep the weak day
　　　moon company and

the wild moan coming
　　　down from the north

to wrinkle the river
　　　and muss the maples

and beeches. When the
　　　last person had gone

inside, the gull dove and
　　　splashed on the ground.

Tired, it sat and watched
　　　with curiosity the grey wad

of paper twitching
　　　open like the egg

of a bird about to hatch,
     a bird that in time might

sing to us about love
     and good intentions

and how little we
     ever know about both.

BEFORE THE AIRPORT, SUSHI

The old man sitting out front
on the empty patio eating
fried chicken or something or other,
bought up the block probably and not
from the house of sushi
we were entering,
didn't inspire confidence exactly,
but when you returned
from the wall of fame to our table
with your chopsticks
in the box you decorated
how many years ago I forget,
and told me regulars from way back
need never use the disposable ones,
wrapped in paper like straws,
that are not smooth
like yours that looked polished
and like they were cut from a yew,
unlike my conjoined sticks
that were little more than gargantuan
toothpicks for some race of giants
that I had only to separate
with one clean snap
and prove were foolproof,
only the engineer who had retired
on the patent for the design of my chopsticks
never met a fool such as I
and so the operation was a failure
except for your laughter,

an unexpected development
for which I would have botched the next set
on purpose, and the next,
only our seaweed salad had arrived
and it was time for me, a lifelong worshipper
of the miniature shovel and pitchfork
to stumble across a tiny plate
with my Chinese finger crutches,
only I didn't and before I knew it
my hand was Fred Astaire on stilts
and the seaweed salad was gone,
followed by half the maki,
and there was only the one pink piece
that separated from the crunchy roe
and its rice wheel that I spit out
because it felt like a tongue
and tasted of death,
which makes perfect sense
because it was dead,
and had our meal ended there,
I would now be celebrating
the virtues of keeping an open mind
to new food, instead of how
life can surprise us so much one day
I'm not eating maple syrup on a steak
or cheese by the block like everyone
who's never been to Vermont
would expect, rather sushi
and mastering chopsticks and looking up
to see a golden braid of hair
I had never noticed was golden
unraveling against your shoulder

so slowly that it looks alive
so much that for a moment
there are suddenly three of us
at the table: me, you, and your braid
that you don't seem to care
is losing what only a few minutes
before I would have called a battle
with gravity, except now I understand
the pull of the earth
isn't always harsh and impatient,
that it can be gentle, can nudge
a twist of hair loose
and in so doing, slow down time
and that song about goodbyes
and the heavy wrap of winter
that fills the sky of every airport town
in late summer, slow that music
down just enough to make a soul
with two left feet like my own
jump up and dance.

FOR MY DAUGHTER

Even after I add up all your birthdays
I've celebrated but that haven't come
to pass since that day long ago when we agreed
it would be better if you never drew that
first breath of air, you're still only zero,
as all the unborn are, though you never look
like a zero, which resembles the eye of a needle
or even less than that, the head of a needle
maybe, though that also seems too large,
which doesn't matter because I always see you small
and running (at what age does that happen?)
across a porch toward my arms
that for once aren't heavy with books or groceries
or even the arms of a lover and as you
draw closer I see your brow is sweaty
because you've been pretending you're a cowboy again
as you like to do, and that I'm a buffalo
stabbed and shot so many times it doesn't know
it's already dead and so it keeps on
limping around while you chase away
the buzzards it thinks are pretty
and so round and round our little game goes
until you get tired of playing the hero, throw
away your star, and face my shaggy frown
just before you smile and jump
back home in between my horns.

RED HERRING

I say "my love" in a reluctant French,
even though I hate the French, not the people
who never did me harm, just the nectar-hearted
sounds of *mon amour, ma chérie,* that always
live in the right mouth on the brink
of tumbling into beauty, a sad truth
revealed to me when I overheard a socialite
ordering a café noisette on the Champs-Élysées
with the same river of honey
spilling from the lips of a street vendor
offering directions to the nearest toilet.
With all apologies to the French, I'm deaf
and dumb to harmony, unless it's guttural,
which is my shortcoming, one of many to be sure,
and so to the reader whose uncle dresses hair
in Marseille or whose grandparents sell tires
or blue eggs or both in the wards of Haiti
and New Orleans and Algeria, dear reader,
to you who wonder why my tin ear
even bothered with your native tongue
instead of following Romeo's lead
and saying O teacher of bright torches, or Goethe's
Die Leiden... for that matter, which is no less accurate
no matter how you translate sorrows,
my whole point was to use a romance
language to persuade you *cher lecteur*
that this is really a poem about love,
and not smoked fish or the vagaries of words,
although one could love a herring

I suppose if the timing were right and the moon
shone just so and the fish could order a pizza
for two in near perfect French,
which I could never do over the phone
in any language without repeating myself,
but which my elegant herring would have no trouble
doing on account of her thinner lips
and mezzo-soprano that has the power to save
some pitiful soul from the torture
of wrestling my mumbled request for black olives,
mushrooms, pepperoni, from English into English.

LITTLE ROAD

For all that is lost in translation,
when the French say *ruelle*
and we say *alleyway* or *bystreet*
on our side of the pond, as the Brits call it,
there is still the same reaching
of the tongue for that pink ridge
above our upper teeth
that every linguist and dentist knows
as the alveolar ridge. Say *little road*
slowly, deliberately, and feel
the wet muscle in your mouth
stroke your gums. If the soft
touch of the tongue to your jawbone
were the only gesture
carried between each language
every time I gave directions
on how to bypass the busy streets
of Paris or Philadelphia,
then this would be a boring study
of coincidence. But I forgot the pucker
the lips must make so the air
passing through them will bend
and become *rue* and *way* and *road*.
Because of this convergence
of sound, when I miss you
I never need to hail a cab
driven by someone from Luxembourg
or the Congo and pay them extra
to take me down every side street

on the way to your home.
No, I only have to wander into any market,
spread my arms, and wait for the crowd
to blow me so many kisses
with every *r* and *l* and *w* they speak
that I look like a tree made of butterflies
at the far end of a small and bustling road
I have come to call my life.

ECHO

That time your hand worked the gearshift
of your Echo that was the color of snail
silver just after the first minutes of daylight
have gone and their trails are no longer
that showy shine of flatware or tinsel,
but the dull grey of the sledgehammer
in your trunk that unlike some people only
moves deliberately and when it has purpose,
just as we were moving that afternoon
when you pointed east, or was it west,
at the famous Camel's Hump of Vermont and said,
It looks like a sitting lion, which it does,
and before it was out of sight, the ashes
of your grandparents and how their spreading
on the mountain was still unfinished
was on your mind was what we talked about,
as well as how long the hike would take and what
I haven't told you is how I've been carrying
that lion in my head ever since that day and how
I finally understand the desire to have one's
body consumed by fire until it is almost as light
as a flame. *What more is there?*
you once asked me. Who needs a heaven,
I say, when your loved ones can nestle you
into a backpack and climb a misnamed mountain
while they talk about the birthday cakes
you baked or the warm barrels
of burning trash on winter nights or
any number of other memories, which

when mixed with their laughter will blend
into a warm note like the kind the strike
your father's hammer makes in the woods
and if the acoustics are just right
that sound made up of a single family
laughing and remembering will echo
and rumble so loudly you would believe
it could reach two people heavy with the weight
of their ancestors riding in a car
miles away and moving slow enough
so that when they stop watching the road
for a moment and look at the great green cat
on the horizon, they would not be surprised
one bit if it yawned, rose, and moved around
like every other living thing.

STARGAZING

I used to walk like a sloth, eyes
on the slow ground, memorizing
every pair of shoes in the seventh grade
until I could name my classmates
by their dingy Keds and George Strait
shit-kickers, the small army of Jordan
sneakers, the suede Airwalks
with the duct tape. There was a way
I moved then, prehistoric
you might call it, that I don't move now,
not since life taught me patience
never filled a hungry stomach or slowed
the sure fist of a bully
whose path would one day cross
with the proverbial tortoise who would
go squish under his tire. Splat and squish
is how the world ends
sometimes. For others, it's like the hiss
of water on a campfire, the steam
rising like ghosts. But where
does it all go? Before long the tortoise
is food and turned into bright
buzzard shit and the steam
from the campfire is even less than that.
I'm tired of living like a rabbit,
all vigor and twitches, bumping
into the world in my hurry
to move through it. And the tortoise,
I don't want to be the tortoise either,

proud of his wit and snail pace
and that living roof
he can never get out from under.
Forget racing, I want to live
slow with no understanding of what it means
to wait. I want my life to be two elephants
dancing in moonlight
without a person in sight. And if not that,
then a pine tree, a bristlecone
like the ones in Nevada
that were needling the sky before people
broke their backs on the pyramids
or a book was needed to justify the ways
of man to man. Let's drive
to Great Basin and spend an afternoon
in the company of that ancient grove.
We can hug and talk
with them about how we've invented
new words for war, and money,
and how even though we now live longer,
we've mastered the art of dying, a fact
that would make a tree laugh
if it could. And let's gather the deadwood
we find, because I want to build
you the tree house you always wanted
as a child. We can make a floor and walls
but no roof so that when it's finished
we can lie side by side at night
in the oldest house on Earth
and you can show me how the outlines
of the stars match the spears of wheat
inked on your torso, the state

of Vermont on your calf, even the lines
by Frost that hug your ribs, the Dickinson
snug against your thigh. And because we are forgetful
we'll have to repeat this every night, slowly,
so slow we'll swear we can feel the tree
in whose young arms our house will sit
pushing new rings into the future,
into a time when I can look at the night sky
and not feel lost, or alone,
because for once everything warm and mortal
about the heavens will make perfect sense.

GOLD RECORD

Dark was the night the *Voyager* slipped
into space carrying the music of one whale
greeting another, as well as the thud
of the stubborn heart and three,
maybe four, people laughing, the sum
of whose voices isn't that much different
from the few seconds of herded sheep,
at least to my poor, imperfect ear
that still has trouble distinguishing
a caterwaul from a stabbing victim,
two sounds our wise Sagan
did not include on his gilded handshake
to the stars, which is regrettable
because what better way to capture
our tempers and apathy than record
some pitiful soul, hand at his punctured
side, trying to groan louder than the TVs
the neighborhood keeps turning up
because they think he's a pair of cats
fucking under the luminous stars,
the very stars the *Voyager* will photograph
on the sly until it stumbles upon a ship
piloted by a race of beings so starved
for connection they cancel their plans
for the evening and sit on shag rugs —
their favorite souvenir from the seventies
— and cue our golden record
on the turntable they inherited
from their in-laws and never expected to use

for anything other than drinks and magazines
to entertain the occasional visitor, much less to hear
Blind Willie Johnson, that priest of the night
Sagan placed alongside Stravinsky
and company because in the three minutes
and twenty-one seconds Johnson sang for Columbia
in 1927 he moaned to the heavens
about homelessness or immortality or some
other mumbo jumbo any race smart enough to escape
gravity and cross the peacock-black
of galaxies would never believe because they
would know the blues are always about love
gone cold, and its light, the clammy light we might spend
years saying we can't live without and then do.

NOTES

PAGE 4

Edward "Wahoo" McDaniel (Choctaw-Chickasaw) played in the
AFL and was a star of professional wrestling during the 1970s
and '80s. One of his legendary feuds was against the flamboyant
"Nature Boy" Ric Flair.

PAGE 5

Saudade is a Portuguese word with no real equivalent in English.
"Andrade" refers to the great Brazilian poet Carlos Drummond de
Andrade.

PAGE 9

Greta Garbo was a film legend of the 1920s and '30s. Arthur Rim-
baud was a French poet whose work revolutionized poetry.

PAGE 13

The first two lines quote the legendary Son House's song "Down-
hearted Blues." Line 4 quotes from the first monologue of his 1965
concert at Oberlin College, in which he shares how love is what
the real "B.L.U.E.S" are all about.

PAGE 18

"Calle a calle" is my translation of what is arguably Pablo Neruda's
best-known and most translated poem, "Walking around."

PAGE 25

"Carità Americana" is a play on the old Roman story of Carità
Romana.

PAGE 36

The lines in quotation marks are my pretending to quote the naïve kind of poetry I wrote when I was younger.

PAGE 38

Sing Sing is a maximum-security prison in Ossining, New York.

PAGE 68

Since 1977, each of the two NASA *Voyager* spacecraft has carried across the galaxy a copy of the Golden Record, a collection of sounds, images, and music representing our planet.

ACKNOWLEDGMENTS

My thanks to the editors of the following publications in which these poems appeared.

AGNI Online: "The Shore Party"

The American Poetry Review: "The Food Critic"

At Length: "Sing Sing"

Blackbird: "Echo"

Connotation Press: "Weekend Home"

Miramar: "Stargazing"

New England Review: "Gold Record," "Red Herring"

Oranges & Sardines: "Dance Couple"

The Paris-American: "Circus Pony," "Grinning in Sardinia"

Ploughshares: "For My Daughter"

Poetry: "Love Train," "Nature Boy," "Salad Days"

Poetry Northwest: "Nudist Colony"

The Southern Review: "Carità Americana"

32 Poems: "Saudades"

"At the Supermarket," "Little Road," and "Patient Zero" originally appeared in *Narrative* magazine.

"Before the Airport, Sushi" appeared in the Poem-a-Day program of the Academy of American Poets.

"Dance Couple" was reprinted in *Driftless Review.*

"Red Herring" was reprinted on *Poetry Daily.*

Much gratitude to my communities at Texas State University, the low-residency MFA program of Vermont College of Fine Arts, and the Bread Loaf Writers' Conference for their support.

Endless thanks to Michael, Kelly, Tonaya, Valerie, Elaina, and the rest of the Copper Canyon family for your faith and the magic of your hands and minds that made this book a thing we can hold.

So much gratitude to Erin Evans, Natalie Díaz, Emilia Phillips, Jessica Smith, Alan Shapiro, Maggie Blake Bailey, Michael Homolka, Dara Barnat, Elizabeth Schmuhl, Mike Croley, Dolores Alfieri, Josh Lopez, Erika L. Sánchez, Katie Kapurch, Vievee Francis, Sunil Yapa, Reese Okyong Kwon, Michael Collier, and Peter Campion, as well as Marie Mockett, James Arthur, Hasanthika Sirisena, Kara Candito, Celeste Ng, Dave Lucas, Elena Passarello, and the rest of the Voltron tribe. To all my friends near and far, the light of your smiles keeps my days lit.

C. Dale Young, Traci Brimhall, David Tomás Martínez, Melissa Stein, and Tom Sleigh all helped me find the shape of this book in spite of some spirited resistance. Whatever faults it may have are mine alone.

To my first and last reader, Micah: my heart, my tonic, now and always, you are the sweet medicine I didn't know I needed.

ABOUT THE AUTHOR

Tomás Q. Morín is the author of *A Larger Country,* winner of the APR/ Honickman Prize. He translated Pablo Neruda's *The Heights of Macchu Picchu,* as well as the libretto *Pancho Villa From a Safe Distance.* With Mari L'Esperance he co-edited *Coming Close: Forty Essays on Philip Levine.* He teaches at Texas State University and in the low-residency MFA program of Vermont College of Fine Arts.

Poetry is vital to language and living. Since 1972, Copper Canyon Press has published extraordinary poetry from around the world to engage the imaginations and intellects of readers, writers, booksellers, librarians, teachers, students, and donors.

WE ARE GRATEFUL FOR THE MAJOR SUPPORT PROVIDED BY:

THE PAUL G. ALLEN
FAMILY FOUNDATION

the POINT
envision·enact·evolve

CULTURE

golden
lasso

Lannan

OFFICE OF ARTS & CULTURE
SEATTLE

WASHINGTON STATE
ARTS COMMISSION

TO LEARN MORE ABOUT UNDERWRITING
COPPER CANYON PRESS TITLES,
PLEASE CALL 360-385-4925 EXT. 103

WE ARE GRATEFUL FOR THE MAJOR SUPPORT PROVIDED BY:

Anonymous

Donna and Matt Bellew

John Branch

Diana Broze

Janet and Les Cox

Beroz Ferrell & The Point, LLC

Mimi Gardner Gates

Linda Gerrard and Walter Parsons

Gull Industries, Inc.
   on behalf of William and
   Ruth True

Rose Gummow

Mark Hamilton and Suzie Rapp

Steven Myron Holl

Lakeside Industries, Inc.
   on behalf of Jeanne Marie Lee

Maureen Lee and Mark Busto

Rhoady Lee and Alan Gartenhaus

Ellie Mathews and Carl Youngmann
   as The North Press

John Phillips and Anne O'Donnell

Joseph C. Roberts

Cynthia Lovelace Sears and
   Frank Buxton

Seattle Foundation

Kim and Jeff Seely

David and Catherine Eaton Skinner

Dan Waggoner

C.D. Wright and Forrest Gander

Charles and Barbara Wright

The dedicated interns and
   faithful volunteers of
   Copper Canyon Press

Printed in the USA
CPSIA information can be obtained
at www.ICGtesting.com
JSHW011257180424
61428JS00013B/172